CHARITIES IN

RESPONDING TO EMERGENCIES

Anne Rooney

www.raintreepublishers.co.uk
Visit our website to find out
more information about
Raintree books.

To order:
☎ Phone 0845 6044371
🖩 Fax +44 (0) 1865 312263
📧 Email myorders@raintreepublishers.co.uk

Customers from outside the UK please telephone +44 1865 312262

Raintree is an imprint of Capstone Global Library Limited, a company incorporated in England and Wales having its registered office at 7 Pilgrim Street, London, EC4V 6LB – Registered company number: 6695582

Edited by Andrew Farrow, Adam Miller, and Diyan Leake
Designed by Victoria Allen
Picture research by Ruth Blair
Illustrations by Oxford Designers & Illustrators
Production by Victoria Fitzgerald
Originated by Capstone Global Library Ltd
Printed and bound in China by Leo Paper Products Ltd

ISBN 978 1 406 23848 8 (hardback)
16 15 14 13 12
10 9 8 7 6 5 4 3 2 1

ISBN 978 1 406 23855 6 (paperback)
17 16 15 14 13
10 9 8 7 6 5 4 3 2 1

British Library Cataloguing in Publication Data
Rooney, Anne.
Responding to emergencies. -- (Charities in action)
363.3'48-dc23
A full catalogue record for this book is available from the British Library.

Acknowledgements
The author and publisher are grateful to the following for permission to reproduce copyright material: Alamy pp. 25 (© Kathy deWitt), 41 (© vario images GmbH & Co.KG), 42 (© International Photobank), 53 (© Bart Pro), 55 (© Adrian Sherratt); Corbis pp. 4 (© Yuan Man/Xinhua Press), 9 (© James Robert Fuller), 11 (© Howard Davies), 16 (© Christophe Calais), 20 (© Howard Davies), 30 (© Andrew Holbrooke), 34 (© Patrick Robert), 36 (© Stephen Morrison/epa), 46 (© Jawed Kargar/epa), 51 (© Marcus Gyger/Reuters); Getty Images pp. 6 (Paula Bronstein), 15 (STR/AFP), 18 (Joe Raedle), 22 (Seyllou/AFP), 28 (Claude Mahoudeau/AFP), 27 (Jewel Samad/AFP), 33 (Esdras Ndikumana/AFP), 39 (Peter Parks/AFP), 44 (Paula Bronstein); © SOS Children p. 48.

Cover photograph of rescuers from Chongqing Municipality saving a survivor in debris of collapsed buildings in Beichuan, one of the counties that suffered the most from an earthquake in south-west China's Sichuan Province, reproduced with permission of Corbis (© Chen Xie/Xinhua Press).

Every effort has been made to contact copyright holders of material reproduced in this book. Any omissions will be rectified in subsequent printings if notice is given to the publisher.

CONTENTS

Words printed in **bold** are explained in the glossary.

EMERGENCY!

Earthquake, flood, fire, hurricane, **famine**, disease, war... Each year, disasters kill around 75,000 people and affect nearly 200 million more, including 60 million children. People are driven from their homes, lose their **livelihoods** or loved ones, and suffer injury and **trauma** as a result of disasters. Luckily, those affected by terrible events do not have to struggle alone. Hundreds of charities, large and small, are quick to help in emergencies.

Chinese emergency rescue workers in the wreckage of a building in Port-au-Prince, Haiti after the city was hit by an earthquake in January 2010.

Helping hands

Charity workers are often amongst the first on the scene of a disaster, along with the emergency services. They offer a crucial lifeline to the people caught up in the event. The work of charities starts in the hours after a disaster and may continue for months or even years afterwards, as people face the challenge to rebuild their lives and communities. The people who work for charities are driven by **compassion** and an urgent desire to help their fellow human beings.

Some charities work at the "sharp end", helping people in situations who may be fighting for their lives. Others work behind the scenes, organizing care and supplies or raising the money needed to fund the charity's work. They range from volunteers to senior professionals.

Short- and long-term help

Relief work is urgent action responding to emergency situations. It includes rescuing people from danger and giving immediate assistance – medical care, food, shelter, water, and essential supplies.

Development work is longer-term help to build **sustainable**, successful communities. It includes education, developing economies and livelihoods, and reducing poverty and long-term **food insecurity**.

What can happen?

There are around 300–500 disasters each year. Experts divide them into natural and man-made disasters, and further divide these into situations that come on suddenly and those that develop more slowly.

Types of disaster

	Natural	Man-made
Sudden onset	earthquake, hurricane/tornado volcanic eruption storms/floods/**tsunami**	war terrorist attack industrial accident transport accident
Slow onset	famine drought disease **epidemic**	**refugee** crisis political crisis

Not all emergencies are large-scale disasters. There are also small-scale emergencies such as people being lost at sea or in the mountains and deserts, for example.

Floods in Jakarta, Indonesia, 2007

In February 2007, Jakarta in Indonesia was hit by its worst floods in 300 years. Heavy rainfall led to the streets of the city flooding. Around 70,000 homes were flooded and 420,000 people had to move out. Many of the poorest people in Jakarta live in wooden houses along the riverbanks, and were severely affected. Around 190,000 people fell ill with diseases related to the flooding, including **dengue fever** and diarrhoea. International aid organizations helped to supply food and also provided medical care for people affected by illness.

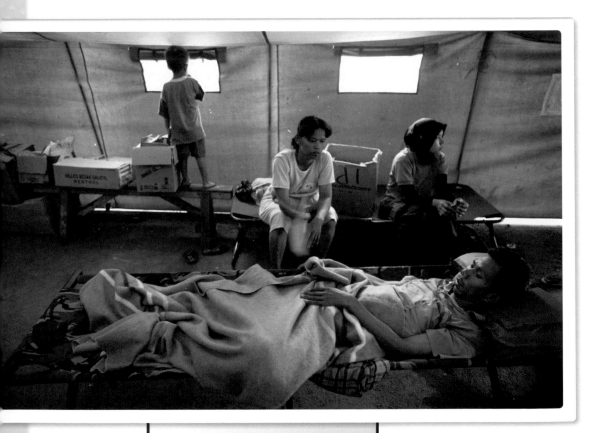

A medical tent set up in Jakarta, Indonesia, to help people affected by flooding in February 2007.

Describing the scene

Warm, brown water and black mud flows through a slum area in Pedongkalan, East Jakarta. It is ankle-deep and carries stinking, rotting rubbish between the tiny houses. The remains of makeshift rafts made from empty water bottles, scraps of wood, polystyrene, and anything else that would float are still lying around, reminders of the flood that has brought such havoc.

One of the houses is a medical clinic funded by the charity Save the Children. People come for free medical treatment for diarrhoea, fever, skin rashes, and eye infections. There are already eight mothers with children queuing outside the clinic before it opens in the early morning. Darini carries her eight-month-old grandchild, Intan, wrapped in a sarong. She describes what happened when the flood came:

> We could not sleep that first night because of the rain and the next day when the floods came we had to leave the house … We did not carry anything because the water was flowing fast so we just wanted to get out of the way. We walked up to the main road and camped underneath the flyover for three days. The police came and gave us a **tarpaulin** and once a day people came and gave us food. On the morning of the fourth day we were told we could not stay there and we had to come back to our house – the water was still up to my neck [around 1.5 metres].

> The main problem before the clinic came was medicine, many children are sick because of the floods and this clinic is crucial if they are to get better again. Intan has had diarrhoea for the last 24 hours.

Another clinic is run by a much smaller, local charity, Hope Worldwide Indonesia. Dr Ita sees patients in the clinic, but one man arrives in great distress because he cannot carry his sick father to the clinic. Dr Ita and his support team rush to the man's home, a small shack made of cardboard. The father is suffering from tuberculosis, a very serious lung disease. They give him suitable medicines and arrange for extra food supplies to be sent to him the next day.

Working with emergencies

Disaster experts talk of four stages in managing emergencies.

Mitigation involves trying to prevent an emergency situation occurring, or limiting the damage it can do. For example, building flood barriers helps to prevent flood damage, and keeping stocks of food helps to guard against famine. Mitigation work undertaken by charities includes educating people in hygiene to avoid the spread of disease and ensuring secure food through stable farming practices.

Preparedness means being ready for a disaster if it does occur. This might involve preparing emergency **evacuation** plans, building shelters, educating people in how to act during natural disasters, training people in rescue work, and keeping emergency equipment ready and available. Charities have their own preparedness plans and strategies so that they are ready to act immediately.

This diagram illustrates the four stages in managing emergencies.

The *response* phase happens when an emergency arises. It includes the immediate rescue work, anything that can be done to limit damage, moving people from the affected area, and bringing in the people and supplies needed to help those affected. Charities work on the front line in the response phase, putting their plans into action and drawing on their preparations.

Recovery can be a long stage, involving rebuilding lives and communities over months, years, or even decades. Charities are heavily involved in recovery work after disasters and emergencies. A good recovery involves mitigation work – learning from the disaster and rebuilding communities in a way that will reduce the impact of future events. For example, making buildings that will withstand earthquakes can reduce the damage caused in future quakes.

This book will concentrate on the work of charities in the last two of these stages: response and recovery.

Being prepared

St John Ambulance is a major international charity. In 2009, local St John staff delivered free disaster-preparedness courses in seven Caribbean countries. They showed people how to create a family emergency plan and put together a 72-hour emergency pack, how to act during different types of disasters, what to do after a disaster, how to carry out basic first aid, and how to cope when a lot of people are hurt. Trainees returned to their communities and trained further people.

A review after Hurricane Tomas struck the island of St Lucia in October 2010 revealed that the preparedness classes had helped people cope during the disaster, minimizing casualties and serious consequences.

"The positive impact that this training has had on the people who've been trained is overwhelming ... [People] ... relate their stories and express gratitude ... We need to continue as this information is necessary to saving lives."
Glenn Wilson, Disaster Preparedness Trainer, St Lucia

Local people help with reconstruction work in the Kampung Jawa district of Banda Aceh, Indonesia, after a tsunami in December 2004 left 500,000 people homeless.

Who works for charities?

The most glamorous image of charity work is of people giving life-saving help to victims of disasters, working heroically in terrible conditions. That is certainly one aspect of charity work, but it is not the only or even the typical experience. Behind the people working in the field is a large group of others working to bring the charity's work to the attention of the public, and raise funds.

Lots of charities compete for the money people are willing to give. Many people work in communications and design, coming up with imaginative and attention-grabbing ways of presenting the charity's message. It has to be easy for people to give money, and charities need to explain how their money will be used. Charities also need managers, administrators, accountants, fundraisers, and people to manage charity shops and organize campaigns – there is a huge variety of work.

Giving

In 2009, just over £9.3 billion was given in aid to help those affected by emergencies. This includes money from government aid funds, corporate gifts, and charities.

There are many different types of charity worker. Some people are volunteers, giving their time for free to a cause they consider worthwhile. Others work in full- or part-time paid employment for charities. There is also a large bank of people with particular skills who are available on standby. Doctors, engineers, and firefighters are amongst the experts who may register with international organizations and fly out to help in disaster areas when necessary. They have arrangements with their usual employers that allow them to take time out to do relief work.

It is not always easy to raise funds for an emergency response, especially if there have been several emergencies in a short space of time. Many people feel there is a lot of pressure to give to one cause after another, and they either cannot afford to or lose interest.

Difficulties raising funds

"Where there is a lot of publicity in the media about an appeal, it is harder to get people to sign **pledges**. *Sometimes they are really rude when we ask them. At the moment, the famine in East Africa is all over the place. People have already given elsewhere, or they don't want to give, and they don't like us asking them."*

Luki, a shop and fundraising volunteer with Oxfam

Rwandan Red Cross workers register refugees who have fled to Zaire during the civil war between Hutus and Tutsis.

Working together

There can be problems when charity work brings help from the outside world and imposes it without regard for the wishes or lifestyles of the recipients. Today, most charities work in a way that is cooperative and enabling. Relief work aims to help people to help themselves – to meet their immediate needs, to rebuild their lives and communities, and to shape their futures as they want them to be. Relief organizations try to support the local economy and use local labour and **expertise**. This helps communities to regenerate economically and to retain a sense of pride and ownership.

Listening

Charities consult with those affected by a disaster to find out what they need, and help them to get it. When helpers from outside a community do not listen to local people, they can make terrible mistakes that waste money and may even cost lives. This means giving people information and choices, listening to what they want, and helping them to achieve it.

> "A lot of aid which has been coming in latterly is I'm afraid ... not very useful. For instance there was a container full of teddy bears ... We do not need rice, we are expecting a bumper harvest, anyone who sends rice is wasting time and money."
>
> Lakshman Kadirgamar, Foreign Minister of Sri Lanka, 2005, referring to donations to help people affected by the Indian Ocean tsunami of 2004

Earthquakes or pigs? Haiti, 2010

Camp Terrain Accra is a large relief camp in Port au Prince, Haiti, which shelters people left homeless by an earthquake [see pages 16–18]. A **psychologist** from the American Refugee Committee supports children coping with the trauma of the earthquake. The team asked the children to draw what frightened them. They expected to see pictures of collapsing buildings and rubble, but 80 per cent of the children drew the pigs that roamed the camp. The pigs were large and sometimes aggressive, and the children were afraid the pigs would attack them. As a result, the camp staff built fences to keep the pigs away from the school area and the children. Without information from the children, it would not have occurred to the camp staff that this was necessary.

Reaching for a future

The people caught in a natural disaster are ordinary people with the same concerns, hopes, and ambitions as everyone else. Natural or man-made disasters can happen in any part of the world. In recent years, Africa has been hit by famine, disease, drought, and war; New Zealand, the Caribbean, India, and Pakistan have suffered earthquakes.

South East Asia and Japan have been hit by tsunami and earthquakes; Asia and the United States have been struck by hurricanes; Australia, the United States, and Europe have had large wildfires; and Europe, Asia, India, and the United States have had terrorist attacks.

People affected by disasters want their lives to return to normal as far as possible, with homes, jobs, and families. Relief work is directed towards this future and treats survivors with dignity and as partners. Jehangir Malik, UK Director of Islamic Relief, reported:

> [Before the floods, people] were living off the land which they used to till and crop and **cultivate** and work … they used to be able to earn their livelihood… The long-term need is that these people [have] a sustainable programme which can help communities get back onto their feet again. They'll need to be working this land once again and that's where the rehabilitation will be required.

This map shows where some of the major emergencies of recent years have occurred, including wars and terrorist attacks as well as natural disasters. The purple shading shows the area affected by the 2004 tsunami.

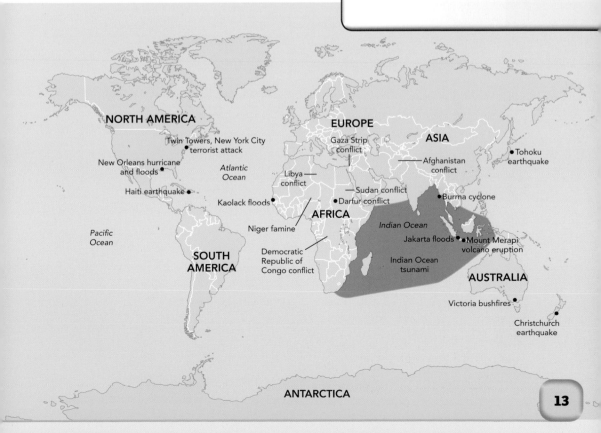

NORTH AMERICA

Twin Towers, New York City terrorist attack

New Orleans hurricane and floods

Atlantic Ocean

Haiti earthquake

Kaolack floods

Pacific Ocean

SOUTH AMERICA

Niger famine

Democratic Republic of Congo conflict

AFRICA

EUROPE

Gaza Strip conflict

Libya conflict

Sudan conflict

Darfur conflict

ASIA

Afghanistan conflict

Tohoku earthquake

Burma cyclone

Indian Ocean

Jakarta floods

Mount Merapi volcano eruption

Indian Ocean tsunami

AUSTRALIA

Victoria bushfires

Christchurch earthquake

ANTARCTICA

DISASTER STRIKES

"The heat surrounded us and there was white smoke everywhere. I saw people running, screaming in the dark, women so scared they fell unconscious. There was an explosion that sounded like it was from a war ... and it got worse, the ash and debris raining down."

Niti Raharjo, survivor of the eruption of Mount Merapi, Indonesia, 2010

Emergency situations can arise in seconds or develop over months. An earthquake, flood, or terrorist attack happens in an instant, but a famine, drought, or war can creep towards a crisis point. Whatever the disaster, people's needs are very similar: food, shelter, clean water, **sanitation**, medical care, and perhaps help with finding their families.

Saving lives

Imagine a scene of total devastation. Buildings have been torn down and people are trapped inside the rubble. Some of the people are badly injured and some already dead. The first rescuers on the scene have to try to remove the trapped people without causing them further harm and without endangering themselves in the process. It can be a painfully slow process, and frustrating for rescue workers who are desperate to get people out as quickly as possible.

Immediate tasks for relief workers include recovering people and bodies from devastated areas; making buildings safe to protect survivors and rescue workers; opening roads and restoring communications links; and dealing with large numbers of displaced, injured, and traumatized people. The urgent need to save trapped or injured people must be met in the first hours and days.

First on the scene

In an overwhelming and sudden disaster such as an earthquake or flood, the road and rail networks are disrupted and it may not even be possible to get helicopters or planes into the area. It might be several hours before anyone can reach the disaster area from outside, and often phone and electricity networks are not working. When a lot of people try to use mobile phone networks and internet, they can fail because there is too much traffic – again making it impossible to communicate with people in the affected area. It is a scene of panic, chaos, and terror.

The very first to offer help to others are usually survivors themselves who are already at the scene. Local and national emergency services such as the police, firefighters, ambulance services, and army usually arrive quickly. Soon after, often within hours, national and international rescue organizations and charities begin to move aid workers into the disaster area.

Worms in the rubble

Finding people buried under the rubble of collapsed buildings is a difficult task. To help, rescuers use lengths of hose 3 metres (9 feet) long and 4 centimetres (1.6 inches) wide, which they can push into the rubble. The end of the hose has a camera or breath sensor to detect people. A designer at the University of Leeds has produced a prototype robot "worm" that could replace the hoses. It can wriggle through the debris, tunnelling through to places that rescuers cannot easily reach. The robot is divided into 12 segments and moves in the same way as a simple **nematode** worm.

Rescue workers using a robot to remove debris. The robot is remotely operated and can lift heavy objects in areas that are dangerous for human rescue workers.

Haiti earthquake, 2010

On 12 January 2010, an earthquake struck in Haiti, centred 25 kilometres (15 miles) outside the capital city of Port-au-Prince. It killed around 316,000 people, injured 300,000 more, and left 1 million people homeless. Haiti is in the Caribbean, occupying the western side of an island shared with the Dominican Republic.

French firefighters of the Detachement d'Intervention de Catastrophe Aeromobile search for survivors in the rubble 24 hours after an earthquake hit the island of Haiti in January 2010.

Rescue mission

Simon Cording is a firefighter. He lives and works in the United Kingdom, but he is also part of the International Search and Rescue Team. He is on standby all the time to be flown out to disaster areas to rescue people. He was summoned by text message to go to Haiti following an earthquake there in 2011. After getting the message in the morning, he flew to Haiti at midnight – he keeps a bag packed and ready all the time. He saw the extent of the devastation as soon as he arrived at the airport near Port-au-Prince. The wrecked landscape stretched on and on; the rescue team drove for hours and saw scenes of destruction all around, constantly.

Simon recalls: "As we walked out, there were bodies strewn all over the streets. Literally piles of bodies – you couldn't look anywhere without seeing something you didn't want to see. People were sleeping on pavements, in the street, and in parks... Haiti looked like the end of the world. And the devastation was relentless: you'd drive for hours and hours, and it didn't end."

People who had lost everything of their own were keen to help move rubble, drive rescue workers around, or act as translators for them. The rescue team first searched the ruins of a church. A service had been taking place when the earthquake struck, and so the church had been full of people. Many had died. But as Simon said: "We had to remember that we were there looking for live casualties; if we got bogged down with body recovery, we would never get anything else done."

On the first day, someone asked Simon's team for help with pulling a small girl from the rubble of a nursery. The whole building had collapsed and two-year-old Mia was trapped in the basement. After four hours digging through rubble, the rescuers could hear her and were able to pass drinks to her. Dehydration is dangerous, especially for a small child.

Finally, after more tunnelling through the collapsed building, a line of rescue workers crawled into the small hole they had excavated. They passed the girl from one to another until she was reunited with her mother. Although it was a happy reunion for them, the team was aware of the grieving parents around whose children had not been recovered alive; six children's bodies lay near by.

Simon is used to confronting death in his rescue work, but even he was shocked at the sight of **JCBs** shovelling thousands of dead bodies into a mass grave.

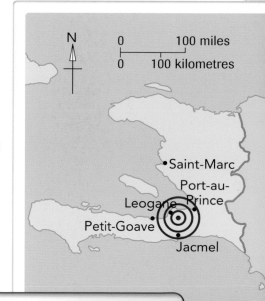

This map shows where the Haiti earthquake struck and how close its epicentre was to dense centres of population. This contributed to the high death toll.

Struggling through

Aid efforts in Port-au-Prince, Haiti, were held up by damage to roads, and by shortages of fuel in the area resulting from damage to petrol stations and increased demand. Alistair Clay of Plan International said that access to the city was a nightmare, and that fuel shortages made it very difficult to deliver emergency supplies: "We are really limited in how far we can drive at the moment because we haven't got enough fuel." Although Plan International had thousands of mobile water tanks available for earthquake victims, delivering them to people in need was very difficult.

If aid cannot get through, frightened people panic and sometimes fight, loot shops, and mob the relief vehicles when they do arrive. In Port-au-Prince, troops dropped water bottles from helicopters because crowds of desperate people blocked the landing areas.

Safety first

When buildings have been destroyed there is a lot of dangerous debris, and remaining buildings are often unsafe. Moving anything can shift other rubble, possibly crushing people who are buried and trapping or injuring rescue workers. At night, rescuers need **generators** and floodlights. Sometimes, rescue attempts must wait until the area has been assessed and made safer by engineering experts. Every minute counts: more people will die the longer the rescue is delayed, but moving in too quickly endangers everyone.

Haitians affected by the earthquake in 2010 rush to pick up water just dropped by helicopter.

Making the scene safe: Christchurch, New Zealand, 2011

A massive earthquake shook the city of Christchurch in New Zealand on 22 February 2011. Large buildings collapsed, leaving people trapped underneath them. The damaged buildings remained unsafe, endangering those working to release trapped people and recover bodies. Experts in engineering and construction were brought in to stabilize the buildings, putting large steel tubes into the collapsing cathedral and pumping concrete into the foyer of a large hotel to protect search and rescue teams.

"This is deeply emotional for those people working on this. They do it because they have an absolute desire to help people, to find people to rescue. Crews work 12 hours a stretch through hot days and cold nights, tapping on walls and pushing cameras into remote [corners] ... and it's a very confined space. It takes a special type of person to do that."

Police superintendent Dave Cliff, New Zealand

When disaster strikes

When a disaster occurs, governments and **non-government organizations (NGOs)**, including charities, swing into action. But they do not just rush in without a plan. That would be inefficient and could do more harm than good. A properly managed, structured response to an emergency makes the best possible use of aid resources. It ensures aid organizations do not compete for resources or duplicate one another's efforts, and the staff and resources that are most urgently needed are delivered quickly. This entails different organizations working together.

Search and rescue

Rescuers often have to search in hostile environments for people who are lost even without a natural disaster - maybe at sea or in mountains, or following a storm, **avalanche**, or accident. A mountain rescue team uses helicopters and people on foot to search. If the lost person has a mobile phone or other GPS contact device, it might be possible to contact them or trace them from a signal. If not, a helicopter is the quickest way of searching a large area.

In many countries, search and rescue is coordinated by state or government forces, often with help from volunteer organizations. In a mountain or bush rescue, local volunteers with a good knowledge of the area, search skills, and first aid are essential. In the United Kingdom, Germany, and The Netherlands, sea rescue is managed entirely by volunteer organizations.

Emergency response units

Large charities have disaster response teams on call 24 hours a day. These teams keep stocks of the essential items that will be needed immediately in many disasters – for example, tarpaulins, water cans, torches, basic medical supplies, and blankets.

The Tanzanian Red Cross distributes food supplies at the Benaco refugee camp, Tanzania to people fleeing the Rwandan civil war.

The right things in the right places

Médecins Sans Frontières (MSF) is a charity that provides first-line medical assistance in disasters of all types. It sends **paramedics**, physicians, and surgeons into emergency situations and runs clinics for weeks and even years following a disaster.

MSF has made pre-packaged disaster kits that include a complete surgical theatre the size of a large table. There is also a miniature kit for helping with childbirth, as well as drugs and other medical supplies. These can be flown out to a disaster zone within 24 hours.

MSF has four **logistical** centres in Europe and East Africa, and stores of emergency materials in Central America and East Asia. Thousands of tents, shelter kits, and other non-perishable items are also stored in centres in China and Dubai.

Information, please!

The first step for a charity responding to a disaster is to find out exactly what has happened. Most charities do not have people in the exact location where a disaster occurs, so they need a reliable source of information on which to base their planning. Charity researchers use the AlertNet website (run by the news agency Reuters) and Reliefweb (run by the **United Nations (UN)**), which provide up-to-date details of all emergency situations throughout the world.

A researcher can produce a briefing kit in minutes using the tools on the Reliefweb website. Using database tools, the researcher can assess medical needs, the food situation, and other requirements. The briefing kit is complete in seconds – work that a few years ago could have taken days. The research and planning team can then plan for the charity's response. This involves finding money and transport for all the work and supplies that will be needed. All this work is done from an office, often thousands of miles from the scene of the disaster.

A day in the life of an ERU team: Senegal, 2009

In the summer of 2009, unusually heavy seasonal rain caused flooding in 12 countries. A total of 940,000 people were affected, nearly 300,000 of them in Senegal. Relatively few people died, but many lost their homes and livelihoods.

The Red Cross carried out relief work in Senegal after the flooding. The work focused on distributing emergency supplies; providing water, sanitation, and shelter; training affected people in the proper construction, use, and maintenance of the facilities; giving cash to affected people; and helping to recover livelihoods after the floods.

The relief emergency response unit (ERU) working in Kaolack, Senegal, was made up of American Red Cross and Senegalese Red Cross members. Its most immediate work in the face of the floods was to take part in assessments – working out the needs of the community and deciding how to identify the people who should be helped. The ERU then developed a ration package to be distributed to people in need, organized a list of people who would receive the packages, and chose a place for distributing packages. Careful assessment and planning meant that relief supplies went to the people most in need, and were delivered to them efficiently, quickly, and safely.

Senegalese boys wade through the flooded streets of Dakar after dangerous floods in August 2009.

9 October 2009

9.00 a.m.: The ERU team meets with the local Senegalese Red Cross Society at the local school to be used as the distribution centre. They assess the arrangements for handing out aid packages to 58 families in the village of Tabangoye. Volunteers organize the families as they arrive, making sure they go to the right place. Their identification cards are checked against the list of people registered to receive aid. After they have been verified, a volunteer shows them where to go next – about 350 metres (380 yards) away to the distribution point. Each recipient has a ticket that they show at the distribution centre, and sign to show they have received the package. A simple process like this ensures that the aid goes where it is needed and everyone who is expecting it receives their share.

At the same time, volunteers in the distribution centre are unpacking supplies that have come in and dividing them into relief packages to hand out. This means breaking up bales of blankets and crates of water containers and other supplies and making them up into appropriate parcels for each family.

2.00 p.m.: The relief team contacts the logistics team because they are 420 blankets short. There are 14 bales of blankets marked as containing 130 blankets each, but they only contain 100 each. It's important to check all the supplies coming in to make sure everything bought or given gets to the right place and to people in need. It turns out that the inner wrappers are marked "100 blankets", so it is a packing error, not fraud. The logistics team arranges to send the extra blankets that are needed.

3.30–5.00 p.m.: The relief team, local branch team, and volunteers meet again to update each other on the distribution and complete reports that will be kept to assess the relief work afterwards. Later, charity workers will visit people's homes or shelters to make sure the items are being used properly.

Getting it wrong

Even in countries with a well-developed **infrastructure** that should be able to cope with disaster, things can go badly wrong if there is poor preparation, panic, or confusion about who should be doing what. In August 2005, Hurricane Katrina struck New Orleans, USA. It destroyed the flood barriers that protected the low-lying city from the sea, and the city was flooded.

Evacuation of the city was begun too late, and people could not leave because roads out of the city were blocked. Available vehicles were not used for the evacuation because of worries about insurance liability. People stuck in New Orleans were sent to unprepared and unsuitable shelters, including the Louisiana Superdome sports centre, where there was not enough food, water, bedding, or toilets.

In addition, the aid sent to the city by the Federal Emergency Management Agency (FEMA) was not enough for the people remaining there. The National Guard kept the American Red Cross and other non-government aid agencies out of the area for several days because of safety concerns. For a long period, no organizations were allowed to drop supplies of food and water for the people who were stranded in New Orleans. Violence and looting spread through parts of the city and some of the emergency evacuation centres.

Where does the money come from?

Many charities face a constant struggle to raise enough money to cover their work. When a disaster strikes, there is an urgent need for extra cash that cannot be met from regular donations and fundraising activities.

The Disasters Emergency Committee (DEC) in the United Kingdom is an umbrella organization that brings together 14 **humanitarian** aid agencies. Instead of charities competing with each other to win funds from the public or from government, the appeal is coordinated. This saves money and resources and makes the process as efficient as possible.

When an emergency situation arises, the DEC decides if a campaign is appropriate and then develops its campaign strategy. A launch date is chosen, and the campaign runs at full strength for two weeks. Radio and television stations give the facilities for making and broadcasting appeals for free.

Newspapers run a prominent advertisement for the DEC campaign in the first 48 hours free of charge. It is made very easy for people to give: there is a free phone line, cash machines have an option to donate when people take money from their banks, and the Post Office and banks allow over-the-counter donations. The appeal stays open for six to nine months.

Genuine charity collectors have identity cards and identifying jackets.

Embracing new methods: money from Twitter

Wendy Harman is social media manager for the American Red Cross. She has made sure the Red Cross has an online presence. Her team began to provide widgets, clips, banners, and photos that made it easy for supporters to create campaigns of their own.

The Haiti earthquake appeal proved the strategy worked. Wendy had a group of 30 celebrities who asked their followers on Twitter to spread messages from the Red Cross. Three hours after the earthquake, Harman's team tweeted the phone number for text donations. In less than 48 hours, the American Red Cross had raised more than £21 million, with £5 million directly from texts.

AS THE DUST SETTLES

"I worry that people will forget about us because the water has gone down. We are forgotten about because we are poor and the flood is gone but we still need help. We need medicine, like this clinic, and we need food."

Darini, a survivor of floods in Jakarta, Indonesia

In the days after a disaster, the immediate needs for food, shelter, and clean water must be met in an organized way. The same is true in a slow-onset emergency such as famine. Aid organizations and governments set up temporary centres where people can go for help and receive food, shelter, water, and medications. A new, strange kind of normality starts to emerge as relief work starts to impose some order on daily life amongst the chaos.

The challenge of disease

Not all natural disasters start with a **cataclysmic** event such as an earthquake or flood. Disease epidemics, famine, and drought do not strike as suddenly. Indeed, disease often follows other disasters. When people are living in poor conditions, in transition camps or temporary shelters, or when they are under-nourished, disease spreads quickly amongst them. Extra doctors and nurses are often flown in to supplement the work of local medical staff.

Sometimes new clinics or field hospitals are set up. Civil and sanitation engineers and construction workers are needed to provide clinics, toilet facilities, and pipelines to provide clean water.

Field hospital in Japan

Israeli Defence Forces built a field hospital in Minamisanriku, a village devastated by the Japanese tsunami in 2011. The hospital has surgical, **paediatric**, and maternity wards, an intensive care unit, a pharmacy, and laboratory. Seven Hebrew-speaking Japanese volunteers joined the medical and construction teams to act as interpreters, and local journalists were asked to publicize the hospital so that people knew how to find it.

Disaster medicine

An emergency produces a lot of casualties in a small area in a very short time. It presents very specific problems for healthcare professionals and relief workers who often have insufficient supplies to deal with all the injured people properly. The field of disaster medicine is relatively new, and was only approved as a discrete field of medicine in 2004.

People who specialize in disaster medicine may work with organizations such as the United Nations or World Health Organization, or with large charities such as MSF, St John Ambulance, or the Red Cross. As well as providing first aid and surgical care to injured people, disaster medical care involves dealing with dehydration, **malnutrition**, and starvation – and also such simple measures as handing out water **purification** tablets and mosquito nets to prevent waterborne diseases and **malaria**. People remain subject to the normal illnesses and complaints that everyone suffers from – they still fall ill, get pregnant, and have accidents. They need routine medical care, too.

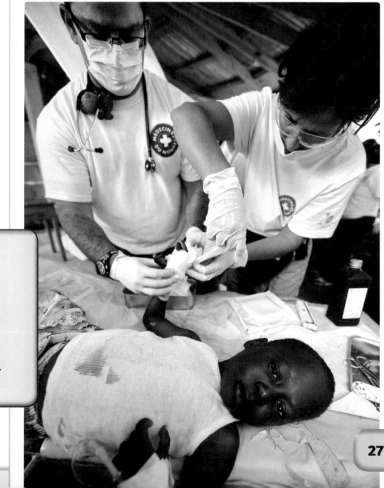

An injured boy is treated at a French-run field hospital in Port-au-Prince, Haiti, following the earthquake that shattered the country.

27

Battling Ebola: Uganda 2011

Ebola is a deadly disease that spreads easily between people. The symptoms are horrific: the body breaks down from the inside, leading to fever, vomiting, headache, joint pain, diarrhoea, and – in the worst cases – bleeding from the eyes, nose, and mouth. Around 70 per cent of people who catch it die.

In 2011, a woman died of Ebola in Uganda. When a second case was suspected, the Ugandan government called on Médecins Sans Frontières for help to prevent an epidemic.

Paul Jawor is a civil engineer working for MSF; he is also a member of RedR, an international register of experts who travel to disaster areas at short notice. He specializes in water and sanitation engineering. He was called to Kaabong in Uganda to try to contain Ebola in June 2011.

The first step for MSF was "line tracing" – tracking down all the people the woman with Ebola had come into contact with in the last few days and stop them mixing with further people. Usually, it is the families and medical staff who tend to the first victims who are the next to fall ill.

An MSF team in Bundibugyo, Uganda, takes a blood sample from someone who may be infected with Ebola following an outbreak of the disease in 2007.

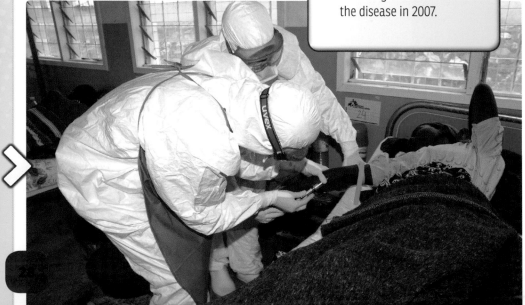

Paul's team had to build an **isolation ward** using whatever materials were to hand in the remote Ugandan village. They used tents, plastic sheeting, wooden poles, and tarpaulins to create a makeshift ward.

A more difficult problem than construction was to work out the logistics of "flow" of people through the isolation unit. To work as a containment unit, each area had to be kept separate – so that people who might have the disease were separated from people who did have it, and from people who had been infected but had not yet developed symptoms. The pathways for health workers and patients to follow had to be carefully laid out to avoid contamination. Engineers erected three sets of fencing around the isolation ward to block it off from passing villagers.

Within the ward, MSF had to tackle the problem of passing infection between people on the clothes of medical workers and through infected waste. Everyone who came into contact with a patient (including family members, doctors, nurses, and the water and sanitation advisers themselves) had to wear protective clothing from head to toe: green scrub-like underwear, overalls, an all-in-one paper suit, goggles, two pairs of gloves, and a plastic apron. When they moved from a high-risk area to a low-risk area, personnel had to remove all this and put on a clean set of protective clothing. Then they were sprayed with chlorine solution to kill any **microbes**. Every door had a chlorine footbath installed.

Disposing of waste was just as challenging. Sanitation engineers had to work out how medical staff would get rid of buckets of infected fluid such as vomit, excrement, or blood, how to dispose of infected clothing and dressings, and even the water used to hose down the ward. Explaining the procedures – and the importance of sticking to them at all times – to local people with no understanding of microbial disease was an equally difficult challenge.

Although the woman died, the medical teams discovered that she did not have Ebola. Paul did not consider the work wasted:

> We left the community with a permanent isolation ward for potential future cases, trained a number of local staff in procedures used to deal with an outbreak and helped protect the villagers of Kaabong from what could have been a very deadly situation.

A day in the clinic at Musasa Camp, Burundi

In 2006 and 2007, 32,000 people fleeing from the Democratic Republic of Congo flowed into Burundi, where they were housed in refugee camps. They were from several different ethnic groups fleeing from civil war, or from violent raids by armed groups, including the Congolese army, Mai-Mai, and Rwandan Interhamwe in North and South Kivu provinces.

The medical clinic in Musasa Camp in Burundi provides emergency medical care to refugees. Many of them are suffering from malnutrition and some have been injured in violent attacks, or on their long journey to Burundi.

A malnourished child is weighed at a medical clinic during the Somalia famine.

The clinic is made of semi-permanent tents put together quickly from available trees and white plastic sheeting. The plastic walls are suspended from wooden poles and the roof is made of metal sheets. There is more plastic sheeting over the ground, and this has to be cleaned each morning. The main doors are made of metal sheets hung in a wooden frame. Bent nails serve as latches. Because the doors can't be locked, all the supplies have to be packed away and moved to lockable storage boxes each night, then brought back out again each morning before the clinic can start work.

The clinic is staffed by MSF professionals and local Burundian people. The MSF team lives an hour's drive from the clinic. The team leader is Carole, a French nurse. Work starts each morning at 9.00 a.m. Carole checks the patients who have been staying in the clinic overnight in the in-patient unit, and talks to the nurse who has attended them. Then she calls a meeting to allocate tasks for the day. The staff regularly switch between tasks and clinics so that everyone develops skills in different areas.

As well as the in-patient clinic, there is a consulting area, a pharmacy, a clinic for dressing wounds, an antenatal (pregnancy) clinic, and a delivery room for pregnant women. Patients coming into the clinic first go to triage (initial screening to decide which patients are in most urgent need). Carole and another MSF nurse check all the children who come into the clinic for malnutrition and fever. Fever is a symptom of malaria, a deadly disease carried by mosquitoes.

Children with fever are given paracetamol. Then they are tested for malaria by a paramedic. He disinfects the child's finger, then pricks it to get a drop of blood. He adds a chemical to the blood that will show in 15 minutes if the child has malaria. The child is sent to sit on a different bench to wait for the results, so that the staff can easily keep track of who has been tested and who is still waiting.

Children who might be **malnourished** are weighed. If they are underweight, a nurse uses a special tape called MUAC tape to measure the circumference of the upper arm. Coloured bands on the tape show the nurse whether the child is malnourished. Some malnourished children can be treated in the camp, but those more severely affected are transferred to a special feeding centre outside the camp.

Crisis management

Many people who come to the clinic have wounds. Two nurses treat and dress wounds constantly, dealing with around 350 patients a day. Some of the wounds start as a rash or sting that people have scratched until the skin has become broken or raw. If it is then covered with a dirty, homemade bandage, it easily becomes infected.

One Burundian woman has grenade wounds. Soldiers entered her house in the middle of the night, killing her husband and wounding her and her son. The woman is in great pain, and is crying and shivering. Carole and another nurse take her to a separate room to dress her injuries. The assistant to MSF's head of mission fills in a report card with details of the woman's story. The report of the violence is essential to both the woman and MSF. The woman can use the medical report if she wants to take legal action, and MSF can use the report to raise awareness of the plight of the people in the camp and get them the help they need.

A little later a nurse asks Carole to examine a girl in a coma. The girl is in the late stages of malaria. She dies after 20 minutes. "Sometimes they wait too long," Carole says. "They don't have transport or money to come in, or they can't leave because they have to work in the field. Now, her mother got neighbours to help her, but it's too late."

Another nurse talks to a group of people in the waiting room about the signs of malaria and how to respond if they see malarial symptoms. All this has happened in the first two hours of the clinic's day.

Some patients need to be monitored for a few days, and they are admitted as in-patients. Nurses watch over the in-patients day and night. If anyone needs care that the clinic cannot provide, the project coordinator of the clinic transfers them to a nearby hospital using a MSF ambulance. The waiting room is full all day, every day, and the clinic treats around 350 patients each day.

Women and children watch government soldiers patrolling an area near their camp in Burundi in 2007. The camp had been attacked by rebels fighting against the government a few days previously.

Somewhere to stay...

When people's homes are destroyed, or they are driven from them, they have to seek whatever shelter they can find. Many have to sleep outdoors, at least for the first few nights after an emergency. If it is cold, this can be dangerous as well as uncomfortable. Relief organizations work as quickly as possible to hand out blankets and plastic sheeting or tarpaulins that can be made into temporary shelters.

A United Nations refugee camp houses 20,000 people who have fled from violence in Libya in 2011. Each tent is equipped with mattresses and blankets.

Suffering

*"It is the elderly who have been hit the hardest. The tsunami engulfed half the town and many lie shivering uncontrollably under blankets. They are suffering from **hypothermia**, having been stranded in their homes without water or electricity."*

Patrick Fuller, International Federation of Red Cross,
Japanese tsunami, 2011

Home from home

Some people move into buildings that serve as evacuation centres, often run jointly by governments, the UN, and charities. In other cases, local people help out, and displaced people can take shelter in real homes.

The kindness of ordinary people who volunteer to help when a disaster strikes is an important contribution in many relief efforts. After a devastating earthquake in Japan in March 2011, a nuclear powerplant at Fukushima was in danger of exploding. Local people were evacuated to a high school that was converted into an emergency centre. Volunteers from the Japanese Buddhist organization Tzu Chi visited the centre, bringing blankets, shawls, nuts, packets of instant soup, and reusable chopsticks and bowls for the refugees.

Helping hands: Libya 2011

Many people fled from violent uprisings against the government in Libya in spring 2011. Around 300,000 Libyans crossed into Tunisia through official border points; of these, 60,000 moved in with generous host families.

Anwar and his wife met a refugee family who had driven over the Libyan border and stopped to buy pastries for breakfast. The couple invited the refugees to stay in their home. Anwar said: "Hundreds of Libyans have been sleeping with their families in their pickups on the sides of the main road in the outskirts of Tataouine. Compassion and **empathy** are not enough to help my Libyan brothers."

A community-based network to support Libyan refugees in Tataouine helped to coordinate refugees and hosts. Host families cannot always afford the financial burden of extra people. The UNHCR (see page 41) committed over £1.8 million to support the host community helping the refugees. Some of the money was spent on improving the health infrastructure to accommodate the extra people. Host families were also given food packages and £22 a month to help with costs.

Food crisis: Niger, Africa, 2005

When people are forced out of their homes at short notice, they take little or nothing with them. They are soon hungry, and there may be nowhere to buy food or no money to buy it with. Food shortages also come about more slowly, with people falling into malnutrition because their food supply fails. Relief organizations need to move quickly to supply food that will not perish and is nutritious.

In 2005 a combination of factors including a plague of locusts that destroyed crops, a drought that reduced the harvest of remaining crops, and extreme poverty, led to a famine in Niger, Africa. Humanitarian organizations set up food distribution centres to supply the food and care that the affected people needed.

Hassan Taifour works for Save the Children as an emergency nutritionist. He worked in a food distribution centre in Niger during the food crisis of 2005.

A malnourished child is fed with special high-energy paste called Plumpy'nut at a clinic run by Médecins Sans Frontières in Ethiopia in 2008.

Hassan said:

> The most important part of our work is to prevent children and adults from dying. When a disaster takes place – when there is an earthquake or a drought or war, when there is **displacement**, refugees, when food security deteriorates and malnutrition rates increase, especially among children under five – that's the time when we are needed. We go to communities and we work with them. We do our best to treat malnourished children, and to prevent those who have not yet become malnourished from becoming malnourished.

Hassan typically worked 12 hours a day at the food distribution centre, starting at 6.00 a.m. and finishing at 6.00 or 7.00 p.m. Sometimes he would need to set off at 4.00 a.m. to get to the distribution centre in time. The main task was to hand out food.

Sometimes they worked after dark, using the headlights of their vehicles or torches, continuing until they were certain everyone had received their ration of food. Paperwork and typing up reports was done in the evenings and at weekends.

Save the Children did not have centres in Niger before the food crisis. It had to set up 12 distribution centres from scratch, each dealing with 1,000–1,500 children. Most of these children would have died without the centres.

Hassan and the other aid workers fed children, distributed food rations to households, and educated the community in health matters. They made a special effort to involve local people in the programme, explaining how it would help them, what problems they would face when it ended, and how they could carry on the care regime that had been set up. They employed people from the local community, mostly women, who went from house to house to explain the programme and measure children to determine whether they were malnourished.

Over the course of the programme, the team reviewed and improved their methods so that, by the end, even severely malnourished children were often treated at home rather than in a clinic. Save the Children aimed to involve the community as much as possible in their own care.

As Hassan said, "Many people from the community get involved and the community feels it is their programme."

Another basic need – information

When a disaster strikes, people outside the area can follow developments on TV, radio, and the internet. However, those inside the area are often left in the dark. **Cyclone** Nargis struck Burma in 2008, killing around 140,000 people. During the days of the cyclone, farmer Kyaw Kyaw and two other families struggled to find £3 ($5) between them so that they could afford a radio to listen to weather updates. They were able to listen to daily five-minute broadcasts made especially for the cyclone-hit areas by the BBC World Service, funded by IrishAid and the Vodafone Foundation.

Information

"*People need information as much as water, food, medicine or shelter. Information can save lives, livelihoods, and resources. Information bestows power.*"

> Markku Niskala, Secretary General, International Federation of Red Cross and Red Crescent Societies

Sharing information

Access to information is essential to survivors. People want to know immediately what has happened, what is being done to help, where to go for aid, and what else might happen. They need to know how to trace relatives, access medical help and relief supplies, register for help and compensation, make nutritious meals from their food ration, and stay healthy. Reliable information helps to reduce feelings of helplessness and loss of control.

It can also help the relief effort. People who know what to do and where to go are easier to work with, less likely to have problems, and more able to help one another. Humanitarian organizations can communicate with people by radio, by leaflets and posters, and by text message, websites, and phone apps.

Sending messages

As well as receiving information, people need to be able to communicate with others. Message boards and mobile phones are a good way of tracing friends and relatives. But in the days after a disaster, mobile networks are over-burdened and often break down. In the hours and days after

Hurricane Katrina hit New Orleans, volunteers from the Amateur Radio Emergency Service provided communications in areas where communications links had been damaged or destroyed.

People also need to communicate with aid workers, and even complain if they are not happy with how they are treated. In the weeks after an earthquake struck Yogyakarta, Java, in 2006, some survivors set up websites detailing whom in their communities had been affected (and how), and what they needed.

Find by phone: Uganda, 2010

In 2010 the charity Refugees United worked together with mobile phone company Ericsson, service provider MTN, and the UN to make a phone app to help people find missing relatives. The pilot scheme was set up in Uganda. There are 127,000 refugees in Uganda, many from the Democratic Republic of Congo. In addition, 250,000 people displaced during civil war in Uganda live in camps.

Behind the app is a database. People can add their own details or search for those of someone else, including name, nickname, date and place of birth, home village, and time and place of last contact. The system is free to use.

Boards were put up, showing details of missing persons at the tsunami crisis centre in Phuket, Thailand, soon after the Indian Ocean tsunami in 2004.

"We are suffering here. The living conditions are difficult. We want to work, we want to live, and we want to move forward. But there is nothing here. We cannot go on and live by begging. This is what we do here – we queue to beg for food."

Emmanuel, 40, Democratic Republic of Congo (in Shousha camp)

Life rarely gets back to normal quickly after a disaster. For many people, a camp becomes home for a long time and all their needs are provided by humanitarian organizations for weeks, months, or even years.

Life in a camp

When houses are destroyed by a natural disaster, it is usually possible to clear away rubble, debris, and perhaps mud and sludge, and then rebuild homes in the same place. But when people are displaced by war, conflict, or climate change that makes their land unusable, they have nowhere to build a new home. These people become refugees, fleeing their homes with nowhere safe to go. Some enter different countries, where they are not always welcome. Many have nothing but the clothes they stand up in. They are in desperate need of help – often hungry, thirsty, and sick after a long and difficult journey.

In the immediate aftermath of a disaster, people struggle to make shelters from tarpaulins or plastic sheeting that will stay up in the wind and rain, or that will protect them from scorching sun. Whenever possible, charities and other aid agencies provide tents, giving people a private space and a more robust shelter. Even so, the tents are closely packed and life is uncomfortable.

Homeless – for how long?

Many refugees end up in camps set up by government organizations, humanitarian aid agencies, and charities. There are around 150 refugee camps around the world, each housing between 300 and 25,000 people – a total of more than 20 million people worldwide.

Camps are intended as temporary homes where people can stay and receive food, water, and medical help. The UN Refugee Agency (UNHCR) aims to repatriate refugees (sending them back to their own land when it is safe to do so), to integrate them into the local community, or to resettle them in other countries. However, many people spend years in refugee camps before they can have a proper home again. This is because many of the situations that lead people to camps take a very long time to resolve.

Roseline Duval, a refugee at L'Annex de la Marie camp in Haiti, says: "They presented me with options and I chose to have a shelter in the camp. I have not yet received a shelter but I will wait as I believe that the Red Cross is doing a good job. I have seen many other people receive shelter, money or have their houses repaired."

People try to get on with normal life in a refugee camp in Butkhak, Afghanistan.

Building toilets: Kalma camp, Darfur, 2010

Violence in Sudan has caused many people to flee their homes. Around 90,000 have moved into a transition camp in Darfur, in the west of Sudan.

One of the first requirements in a refugee camp is for toilets, or **latrines**. Without proper toilet facilities, people are forced to go on open ground, and this can very easily lead to disease. Providing toilets, removing waste, and keeping water supplies clean are the keys to preventing epidemics of deadly diseases such as cholera and dysentery.

A young man helps to build a latrine pit as part of a charitable project in Fort Dauphin, Madagascar.

Oxfam has sent engineers who are experts in mass sanitation to work in the Kalma relocation camp in Darfur. The engineers are in charge of providing latrines. They first discuss the project with members of the refugee community to identify sites that will be suitable – both in terms of the practicalities of digging the ground and being somewhere that people consider safe and easy to get to.

Construction starts by digging trenches. If the ground is sandy, the trenches must be lined with bricks so that they do not cave in. There are plenty of people with little to do in a refugee camp, so it is easy to find volunteers to dig the trenches. Plastic or cement slabs with holes in are laid over the trenches. There is a lid to cover each hole, to reduce smell and improve hygiene. If possible, the cement slabs are made in the camp by the refugees. However, plastic toilet slabs can be imported if this is not possible.

Then dividers are built between the holes to give people some privacy. Wherever possible, these are made from locally sourced materials such as bamboo or rush matting. Charity workers rely on the expertise of the refugees who know the area and are best equipped to suggest suitable materials. The toilet cubicles may not have a roof if the weather is good. Children in some areas are used to spending most of their time outdoors and are afraid of the small, enclosed space of a cubicle. Being sensitive to such needs is important to the project's success.

Once the toilets are built, refugees are recruited to attend and manage them. This means making sure they are used properly and kept clean. Charity workers teach people how to use them properly and give lessons to adults and children in hygiene. They emphasize the importance of washing their hands after going to the toilet. These people then go on to teach another six people, and they teach another six. It is a good way of spreading knowledge through a large community.

Making a normal life in an abnormal situation

It may not sound very important, but a big problem for people living in refugee camps is boredom. People are no longer able to work as they usually do, children cannot go to school, and everyone is living on top of each other. Conflicts and arguments can flare up quickly. Many young people spend their days playing football and other games to pass the time.

Camp organizers try to involve people living in the camp in useful activities as much as possible; for example, running facilities, making things that are needed, and continuing the children's education. If children have no schools, they find it difficult to integrate when they rejoin normal society outside the camp.

Fidel Nshombo became a refugee when his school was attacked and he was separated from his family. He lived for nine years in a series of camps, and was eventually resettled in Boise, Idaho, USA. But at the age of 17 he knew less about daily life than some five-year-olds in his new town. He did not know how to use a computer or a lift, for instance. He found this very embarrassing. However, Fidel eventually settled happily. He works in accounting, enjoys football, and promotes peace. In 2011, he became a US citizen and was reunited with his family.

Men play football at the tent city of Jalozai camp, near Peshawar, Pakistan. The refugees have fled from fighting and face extremely harsh living conditions in the overcrowded camp.

Pretend Camp

When people from a refugee camp are resettled in a new country, it can be difficult for their new neighbours to understand what they have gone through. Cara Winters of the International Rescue Committee worked with volunteers from the Refugee Resettlement Volunteers to stage Camp Refugee in the state of Arizona, USA. It was a mock-up of a night in a refugee camp. Its aim was to give local people an insight into what the 2,000 international refugees resettling in their area had experienced.

More than 50 students played the parts of refugees, UN workers, and human smugglers. After creating their own tents with sheets, wooden dowels, and twine, the "refugees" settled down for a night disturbed by recorded gunfire and the glare of floodlights directed at their tents. When they woke the next morning, some of the "refugees" had disappeared – supposedly victims of disease or murder.

The "refugees" then experienced mock medical assessments and interviews with UN workers, based on genuine field practices. They were given typical rations of crackers and peanuts, and told to use makeshift latrines. Hawa Seangarie from Liberia then described her own experience of 15 years in refugee camps in West Africa to the "refugees", telling them about torture, famine, and resettlement.

"We think we have all these other problems to worry about, but they are really trivial compared to theirs," said Claire Lewinski, who played the role of a Cambodian refugee. "You couldn't trust anybody. You never knew what you were supposed to do as a refugee."

Hostile environments

It is important that humanitarian aid is **impartial**, independent, and **neutral**. It can sometimes be difficult for humanitarian agencies to convince people of their neutrality, and aid has become a political tool in some parts of the world.

In parts of Afghanistan and Iraq, the **Taliban** has suggested that aid from the United States and the UN is an attempt to "buy off" poor Afghani and Iraqi citizens, winning them over from the Taliban in exchange for aid. The Taliban uses this argument as an excuse for targeting aid workers.

In 2009, the terrorist group Al-Shabaab banned foreign aid agencies from operating in Somalia in East Africa. In 2011, the Libyan government prevented aid agencies from getting to people in the west of the country that were in need of help. Pro-government military operations have sometimes used the symbols of the Red Cross and the Red Crescent as a disguise for their own shipments of troops and weapons.

Afghan police at the scene of a roadside bomb that struck a Mercy Corps vehicle, injuring four aid workers. The attack was the work of the Taliban.

Delivering emergency supplies often entails a difficult and dangerous journey. Aid **convoys** may be robbed, or forced to give up a portion of their cargo in bribes. When aid cannot get through, camp officials sometimes have to buy supplies on the **black market**.

Wael Abu Mustafa is director of the SOS village Rafah in the Gaza strip in Palestine. The village had to buy essential supplies on the black market – by illegal trade – when all the shops were closed during conflict between Palestinian and Israeli forces in the area. He reported: "Currently [we have] a two-week supply of basic goods (flour, oil, rice, etc.). We were able to obtain gas, essential for both cooking and heating, on the black market for **exorbitant** prices."

Stand-off over aid row: Sudan 2009

In 2009, the Sudanese government expelled foreign aid groups from the Kalma displacement camp, including Care International, Oxfam, and MSF. The government accused the charities of helping the International Criminal Court build a war-crimes case against the Sudanese president. Al-Hadi Najim, secretary-general of the government agency that oversees humanitarian aid in Sudan, complained that the expelled foreign aid agencies spent too much money on themselves, including guesthouses, security guards, and air-conditioned trucks.

Leaders of the Kalma camp suspected the government and Sudanese charities of spying on them. They rejected all aid deliveries in a protest against the government's actions. This put the 88,000 residents at risk. Food from the World Food Programme and the UN was turned away from the camp, the health clinics shut down, and fuel ran out. A **meningitis** epidemic started, and some people had to fetch water from a polluted river. Food prices rose in the camp's markets.

Al-Hadi Najim was reported to say: "We hope that more people will go home. They can't spend the rest of their lives begging the international community to feed them."

"*Most people are back to living their 'normal' lives, but are doing it living in tents. Some beneficiaries, though, are now living a more comfortable life thanks to support from donors and NGOs. Before the tsunami they lived in very basic huts and now they have solid buildings, water, schools ... This is quite different to what was 'normal' for them, but still, they seem to have adapted well to the changes.*"

Cedric de Silva, Director of SOS Children's Villages, Sri Lanka

Finding their feet

After a disaster, many people have lost their livelihood. In order to stand on their own feet again, they need a home and a source of income. Some people take decisions that make their life better in the short term, but harder in the long term; for example, selling a cow to pay for a funeral. An emergency response unit dealing with people's livelihoods can provide cash grants and training to aid a recovery plan.

Children enjoying lessons in a temporary school set up by SOS Children, in Sri Lanka.

Coping with trauma

It is not just houses, communities, and livelihoods that are wrecked by war, earthquakes, and floods. Lives and families can be destroyed, and need careful **nurturing** if they are to be rebuilt. Charities play a very important role in psychological recovery, as well as in the practical aspects of rebuilding homes and restoring economic security.

After a disaster, many people are very distressed. They might have lost loved ones, their homes, or their communities – or they may have suffered terrible physical experiences. When their suffering has been deliberately inflicted by others, their recovery can be very difficult.

Rape as a weapon: Libya 2011

Hana Elgadi is a Libyan volunteer with a group that offered medical help and **HIV** tests to women who were raped by soldiers and mercenaries during the conflict in Libya in 2011. She said: "It is difficult to persuade those affected to come forward for help because of the shame associated with rape. They will not ask for help with sexually transmitted diseases or pregnancy that result from rape as they are too afraid of the response of their families."

Nader Elhamessi of World for Libya reported that Libyan women are also in danger of "honour killings": "Many fathers will kill their own daughters if they find out they have been raped."

Relief workers must be sensitive to local beliefs and traditions. When local attitudes need to be challenged in order to help people, this must be done from within a system the community trusts. The charity World for Libya flew in an important **sheikh** from the United Arab Emirates to help persuade Libyan women that rape is similar to being shot – not their fault, not a sin, and not something they need to be ashamed of.

Mending minds: Darfur, 2007

Rasha is a psychologist who works at the **psychosocial** relief centre of SOS Children's Villages at Abu Shok refugee camp in Al Fashir, Darfur. She treated a young teenage girl called Farida.

Farida's early life in her farming community was happy. Then one day armed gunmen belonging to a group called the Janjaweed stormed her village. They burned homes, killed livestock, and slaughtered many of the men in front of their families. All the villagers were driven from their homes. Farida and some other young girls in the village were kidnapped by soldiers. Most of them were raped, and then released. They made their way to Al Fashir, where Farida was reunited with her mother and siblings. Together, they moved to Abu Shok refugee camp where they built a tiny mud hut for themselves.

When Rasha started seeing Farida, she was having constant tension headaches, frequent bouts of crying, and nightmares. She was terrified of men, especially light-skinned men who reminded her of the Janjaweed soldiers. She showed signs of depression and **post-traumatic stress**. Like many traumatized young people, Farida found it impossible to express herself in words. Rasha remembers:

> At first I did not ask her any direct questions about her experiences, but asked her to draw, make clay figures, and other forms of expression.

> Gradually I got her to play this game, sort of like a puppet show, but only with one puppet. She then started telling her story to the puppet.

> It was extremely hard for her to adjust. Farida is one of the patients who had to receive medication for her condition, especially because of her constant feeling of terror and panic. Although she did not tell me directly exactly what had happened to her, she spoke about how the other girls were raped and what had happened to them.

Eventually, Farida started to adjust to life in the refugee camp. The peace and security of the camp helped reduce her panic. Her day-to-day activities helped keep her busy so that she did not constantly recall the terrible things that had happened to her. Farida was finally able to return to school. She came to trust Rasha and the other relief workers in the village, feeling that they were there to help her.

Rasha is realistic about how much can be achieved for young people who have suffered terrible trauma: "Generally speaking, the children who come here have been through experiences that remain with them for the rest of their lives. We can only help them accept these experiences and adjust to life. We can't wipe them away."

The refugee camp Abu Shok near El Fasher in the western region of Darfur in Sudan.

From relief to development

Careful planning plays a key role in rebuilding communities after a disaster. The aim is to create an environment that is sustainable, fair, and suited to the wants and needs of local people.

Charities try to buy supplies and materials locally so that they help to support the damaged economy. Sometimes they will give people money rather than supplies. This can be a good choice if there are enough goods in local shops and markets to meet people's needs. It gives them a sense of control, and helps the local economy.

Alwynn Javier, Senior Emergency Programme Officer at Christian Aid in Manila, says: "In these areas where the struggle to survive is a daily reality, cash grants could give them the freedom to address their most urgent needs, whether that is food or any other basic life-saving item."

Charity chickens: Afghanistan, 2011

The International Rescue Committee (IRC) relief teams built poultry shelters and hatchery units for chicks in 12 communities in north Afghanistan. They also provided **incubators**, feeding equipment, and eggs to hatch. The project helps women from 220 families to earn a living. The IRC also trained farmers in managing livestock and looking after farm animals.

Forgotten by the media

"My experience is that as soon as it drops out of the media, the focus moves on, and there is another emergency in the world, yet when that political and media interest moves on, you always have people who are left behind to struggle by themselves. Years later, people could still be living on this border in tents and plastic sheeting."

Andrew Gleadle, International Medical Corps

Helping people to help themselves – long distance

The internet has revolutionized the way that experts in different fields can contribute to relief work. The organization Engineer Aid helps solve engineering challenges for people in need at a distance. Charity field workers contact Engineer Aid to ask for solutions to practical problems that can be put in place by the local people. This involves people directly in rebuilding their own communities, and saves money on transporting materials and people.

A village in Malawi asked for help collecting fresh drinking water. Villagers could collect rainwater as it ran off a roof, but the first water was filled with dust and debris washed from the roof. But when the dirty water had been collected, the metal collection tub was too heavy to move and they could not collect clean water. Engineer Aid designed a system for moving the pipe, not the tub. With a simple swivel, the pipe could direct water into a second collecting tank after the dirty water had collected. The engineer worked in the United Kingdom, and villagers in Malawi built what he designed.

Although the public responds quickly when a major disaster strikes, interest soon moves on while those affected still need help. It is important that even when an emergency is no longer in the news, humanitarian organizations continue to support people.

This woman in Haiti is working on a project set up by an NGO called Habitat for Humanity.

HOW TO VOLUNTEER

"I've been a volunteer for 10 years. First-aid training can save lives.
I was very proud and happy to be putting what I'd learned into practice.
I'm going to stay a volunteer for the rest of my life."

Maguette Baldé, volunteer with the Senegalese Red Cross

Many young people are keen to make a difference in the world by helping others. Working for a charity is a good way to do that, and to feel that you are spending your time on something worthwhile. While most school students are too young for a career in relief work, it is possible to help out by giving time – volunteering either to help directly or to raise money for charity.

Opportunities for young people

How much you will be able to do as a volunteer depends on where in the world you live. Many countries have regulations about the age you have to be in order to act as a volunteer. But do not be put off – there is still plenty you can do.

Charities such as the Red Cross and St John Ambulance run courses in most countries that will train you in first aid. Once trained, and when you are old enough, you can attend local events as a first aider. If you later want to work in relief work, this is a good initial preparation.

Volunteers in the front line

The Black Saturday bushfires started in Victoria, Australia in February 2009 and burned for over a month. St John Ambulance volunteers and trained medical staff from around Australia staffed emergency posts throughout the affected area, giving first aid treatment to civilians and firefighters and moving injured people to hospital.

These junior school children in Bristol are learning first aid skills.

Working locally

Even large international aid organizations have many small local branches that are always looking for volunteers. If you have skills in suitable areas you might be able to help out – for instance, by creating posters or building a website. If you speak more than one language fluently, you might be able to translate for refugees or other people caught up in a disaster situation.

There are lots of tasks that anyone can do, even without any special skills. Anyone can deliver donation envelopes or leaflets, or check that games and jigsaws donated to a charity shop have all their pieces. If you are old enough, you can work in a charity shop during school holidays or at weekends.

Just click!

There is a very simple way that anyone can give a tiny donation to charity. The Hunger Site (www.thehungersite.com) is a website which gives donations to charities working in relief and development areas around the world each time someone clicks on a button. The donations are funded by advertisers – all you have to do is click once a day (you can't click more than once from a single computer).

Raising money

The best opportunities for young people are in raising money. You will not need to look far to find an event you can support or take part in. Whenever there is a major emergency, lots of charities stage fundraising events or encourage the public to raise money for them. You might be able to take part in a sponsored run, a car boot sale, or fête.

You could even organize your own fundraising event or campaign and give the money to a charity helping in a disaster area. Perhaps you could persuade your school to allow pupils to wear silly costumes for a day and give a small donation to charity for the privilege. Or maybe you can arrange a cake sale or a mini-music festival.

Raising money through a charity event

Many charities offer lots of help with setting up your own campaigns and events. They give advice on organizing, running, and publicizing events, lots of ideas to spark your imagination, and often templates and documents you can use to help let other people know about your event. You might be able to register your event with the charity so that they can help publicize it.

You can often set up a web page to make it easy for people to give to your fund, with the money going directly to the charity you have chosen. There may be widgets, badges, and logos you can use on your own web page, blog, or social networking page. For example, the US charity Mercy Corps lets you choose a cause from those it supports and then set up a fundraising page of your own. The advantage to doing this is that you don't need to collect money or handle cash – people give directly to the charity through the web page. It is a useful way of managing money for an event such as a sponsored bike-ride where your supporters don't need to turn up but can support you from a distance.

Don't forget to make a Facebook page, and use Twitter and any other social networks you use to publicize your campaign.

"The most challenging part of working for the Red Cross is responding to disasters. You never know when a disaster will happen so essentially we are on-call all the time. When one does happen, such as Haiti or Japan, it is all-hands-on-deck and our teams work around the clock to respond."

Karen Snider, National Media Manager,
Canadian Red Cross

1863 International Committee of the Red Cross is established in Geneva, Switzerland. The Swiss businessman Henry Dunant was appalled at the suffering of thousands of men who were left to die after the Battle of Solferino in 1859. He suggested setting up national relief societies made up of volunteers who would be trained in peacetime to provide neutral help to relieve suffering in wars.

1877 St John Ambulance Association is set up in the United Kingdom to teach first aid in large railway centres and mining districts. Its origins lie in the Order of St John Hospitaller, which started in 1099. St John Ambulance Brigade was formed to provide first aid services at public events.

1900 The Salvation Army disaster relief starts. The Galveston hurricane on 8 September is the Salvation Army's first major disaster response effort in the United States. Over 5,000 people died. Salvation Army officers help clean, feed, and shelter thousands of survivors.

1906 The Salvation Army's first coordinated, nationwide fundraising effort for disaster relief is launched. Salvation Army personnel establish feeding stations and shelters throughout San Francisco after the city is destroyed by an earthquake and fires in April.

1914–1918 Red Cross tracing and message service is started. During World War I, the Red Cross sets up a service to help trace soldiers injured or missing at the Front. They are authorized to search villages and hospitals for missing people and put them in touch with their families.

1948 Oxfam opens its first shop, one of the world's first charity shops, in Oxford. Oxfam was founded in 1942 to help Greek people suffering from famine in World War II. It now fights poverty around the world, engaging in disaster relief, development work, and campaigning for better working and living conditions for the world's poorest people.

1967–1970 The state of Biafra tries to separate from Nigeria in 1967. During two-and-a-half years of fighting, a million people die from famine and violence. It is the first televised famine, and it sparks an international relief effort as people elsewhere see for the first time the effects of a humanitarian disaster.

1970 Bhola cyclone, the third most deadly disaster of the last 100 years, kills 300,000–500,000 people in Bangladesh (East Pakistan), 12 November. George Harrison, previously of the Beatles, organizes the first large charity benefit concert in response to the cyclone and the atrocities in conflicts in Bangladesh the following year. The Concert for Bangladesh takes place in New York City, USA.

1971 Foundation of Médecins Sans Frontières (MSF, also known as Doctors Without Borders). A group of French doctors on an international aid mission to the Biafran conflict in 1970 become frustrated by government interference in humanitarian aid and what they consider the Red Cross's cooperation with the government. They join up with a group of French journalists and found MSF to provide care that ignores political boundaries.

1984 Band Aid raises money for famine in Ethiopia. Bob Geldof and Midge Ure form a "super group" which releases a single, "Do they Know It's Christmas?" It becomes the best-selling single in the United Kingdom up to that date. There was considerable criticism of the song, the project, and how the money raised was spent.

1999 MSF wins the Nobel Peace Prize.

2001 On 11 September, terrorists attack the World Trade Center in New York and the Pentagon in Washington, DC, crashing aeroplanes into the buildings. Another plane crashes into a field. Nearly 3,000 people die; over 400 of them are relief workers such as firefighters, paramedics, and police officers.

2004 Indian Ocean tsunami on 26 December. Relief organizations from around the world help out. Three of the five other deadly disasters happen inside China while it is closed to international aid organizations.

2010 Haiti earthquake on 12 January affects up to 3 million people, though there is considerable disagreement about the number of deaths. Most people in Haiti speak only Haitian Creole – a machine translator between Creole and English is quickly developed to help aid organizations to communicate with survivors.

2011 An earthquake in March destroys buildings in Japan and also triggers a tsunami that devastates large areas of land. The earthquake damages a nuclear power station in Fukushima, leading to the escape of radioactive material that contaminates the local area and causes illness amongst residents. It is the first time a natural disaster triggers a major nuclear alert, presenting a particular challenge to relief efforts.

GLOSSARY

avalanche dangerous flood of snow falling down a mountain after it has been displaced

black market illegal trade in goods in violation of official regulations

cataclysmic extremely destructive

compassion desire to help someone who is suffering

convoy group of vehicles travelling together for protection

cultivate grow

cyclone very strong, whirling winds that move in a spiral pattern

dengue fever dangerous illness spread by mosquitoes

displacement being moved from the proper or previous place

empathy fellow-feeling or sympathy with someone

epidemic outbreak of a disease in which many people fall ill

evacuation making people leave a dangerous area in order to stay safe

exorbitant extremely expensive

expertise special knowledge

famine severe and widespread lack of food

food insecurity unreliable access to nourishing food

generator equipment for generating electricity

HIV human immunodeficiency virus; condition that causes the body's immune system to break down

humanitarian having concern for or helping people

hypothermia dangerous condition caused by being extremely cold

impartial treating all opinions equally seriously

incubator equipment for keeping something warm, at a stable temperature

infrastructure physical and organizational structures

isolation ward hospital ward that is cut off from other wards to prevent the spread of disease

JCB vehicle for excavating and digging

latrine communal toilet block

logistical relating to the management of the details of an operation

livelihood way of earning a living

malaria dangerous disease carried by mosquitoes; it causes severe fever and can be fatal

malnourished suffering from malnutrition

malnutrition condition caused by not taking in enough nutrients, such as protein and vitamins

mannequin plastic model person used for displaying clothes in a shop

meningitis dangerous illness which causes inflammation of the membrane over the brain and can cause death

microbe very tiny organism, such as bacteria

nematode type of biologically very simple worm

neutral not supporting or helping any particular side or political view

non-government organization (NGO) charity or association that is independent of government or business

nurture look after and encourage to grow

paediatrics field of medicine relating to the care of children

paramedic person who gives first aid or emergency care before proper treatment

pledge promise (to give money)

post-traumatic stress psychological reaction resulting from a deeply shocking experience

psychologist medical expert who deals with mental health and well-being

psychosocial relating to psychological and social state

purification making clean

refugee person who has been displaced from their home and has nowhere permanent to go

relief work work to relieve suffering

sanitation promoting health by preventing contact with waste and dirt

sheikh Arab leader or ruler

sustainable capable of being maintained

Taliban Islamic fundamentalist military group

tarpaulin large sheet of strong, waterproof fabric

trauma deeply distressing event that is very hard to recover from

tsunami flood of sea water that rushes inland resulting from massive displacement of water, often by an undersea earthquake or volcanic eruption

United Nations (UN) international organization of countries set up in 1945 to promote international peace, security, and cooperation

> FIND OUT MORE

Books

The Global Village: Aid and Development, Ali Brownlie Bojang
(Evans Brothers, 2008)

Under the Persimmon Tree, Suzanne Fisher Staples (Walker Books, 2006)
The story of a Najmah, an Afghan child who has to go to Pakistan on foot as
a refugee and then attends a refugee school under a persimmon tree.

Film

Beyond Borders, Martin Campbell (2002), a film set amongst relief work during
an African famine. The representation of charity work has been criticized.

YouTube

Most charities have their own YouTube channels and post videos about their
work, including their latest appeals and footage from places where they are
helping. On the YouTube page, search for the name of the charity you are
interested in, or go to one of these pages:

www.youtube.com/user/OxfamGreatBritain
www.youtube.com/user/oxfamameric
www.youtube.com/user/oxfamaustralia
www.youtube.com/user/savethechildrenuk
www.youtube.com/user/AmRedCross
www.youtube.com/user/MSF

Websites

You can find out about the emergency relief work of these major charities on
their websites. Many have country-specific websites as well as their global
website. Some have interviews with staff members or case studies of their
work. The websites of the organizations mentioned in the book are listed
below. Many have useful information about their relief work.

Disaster Emergency Committee: **www.dec.org.uk**
EngineerAid: **www.engineeraid.com**
Hope Worldwide: **www.hopeww.org**
International Medical Corps: **www.imcworldwide.org**
International Search and Rescue: **www.britishcivildefence.org/International_**
  Rescue_Team/international_rescue_team.html

The International Federation Red Cross and Red Crescent Societies:
   www.redcross.org and **www.redcross.org.uk**
IrishAid: **www.irishaid.gov.ie**
Médecins Sans Frontières (Doctors Without Borders): **www.msf.org.uk**
Mercy Corps: **www.mercycorps.org/fund-raising**
Oxfam: **www.oxfam.org and www.oxfam.org.uk**
Plan International: **www.plan-uk.org**

Topics to research

Charities are not the only organizations that provide aid in disaster zones. Local governments or state authorities provide a lot of help, and the United Nations helps in many emergencies worldwide. These organizations often work in partnership with charities. To understand fully the role of charities in disaster work, you need to know how their contribution fits into the complete picture. Find out what the United Nations does to help children, refugees, and others affected by emergency situations. There is a lot of information on the United Nations website: **www.un.org**.

Besides charities' work with major disasters and emergencies, there are many charities that deal with smaller, local emergencies. Find out about charities like this in your own area. If you live near the coast, for example, there may be a lifeboat service. If you live near mountains, there may be a mountain rescue service. These often use rescue vehicles, including helicopters, to find people who are lost or trapped and take them to hospital. Research the local work of charities such as the Red Cross and St John Ambulance, too.

Although charity workers respond quickly to disaster, local emergency services are usually the first on the scene and play a very important role in rescuing and treating people affected. Find out about the work of the emergency services in situations such as terrorist attacks, natural disasters, and industrial accidents.

ReliefWeb: reliefweb.int
Provides up-to-date information about all current emergency situations around the world and has tools for building a disaster-briefing pack.

AlertNet: www.trust.org/alertnet
Provides up-to-date information about all current emergency situations around the world.

hisz.rsoe.hu/alertmap/index2.php?smp=&lang=eng
A real-time map of disasters happening around the world. Click on a marker to see more details about the disaster.

>> INDEX